Contents

Welcome

This is the Cotswold Farm Park. It's been part of my life for as long as I can remember and I'm delighted to share it with you in words and pictures. I'm proud to say that I'm a true Cotswolder, born and bred among these gentle green hills.

Perhaps you already feel you know the place. After all, every Sunday evening millions of 'Countryfile' viewers see the ups and downs of daily life on 'Adam's Farm'. But what happens when the cameras stop rolling and how does a mixed farm in an ancient landscape operate in the 21st century?

In the following pages you'll find out more about what goes on behind the scenes at the farm, the story of modern agriculture, the fascinating history of Britain's rare breeds and the people who work hard to look after them.

I really hope it gives you an insight in to the rural way of life and an appreciation of the important role that farmers play. Consider this as your personal guided tour to a very special corner of the English countryside.

Happy reading!

Adam Henson

Where it all Began...

Every day is a variety of surprises in this job. I could be helping a nanny goat with a difficult birth, building new pens for the Old Spot pigs or leading the 'Countryfile' film crew through the barley field to explain the ins and outs of harvesting.

The farm sits alongside an old cross country route called Buckle Street which runs from Bourton-on-the-Water to Broadway. It's an old Roman road and there's some suggestion it was even a Neolithic salt way or trading route. The first written record of Buckle Street is in a Saxon Charter of 709 AD where it appears as *Bugghilde Street*.

Cotswold stone has always been a highly valued building material and it's been excavated from the area since the days of the Domesday Book. When you gaze across the bustling animal sheds and paddocks of the Farm Park today, it's hard to imagine that a century ago the site was a working quarry. Some of the stone was used to make Cotswold tiles and it's thought that the roof tiles of Corpus Christi College, Oxford came from here.

The scars of that industrial past were still visible 50 years ago when the Henson family moved to Bemborough Farm and the 10 hectares (25 acres) of uneven pasture were quickly nicknamed the '**Humpty Dumps**'.

I never forget that farming is a way of life which goes back thousands of years in the Cotswolds. Who knows when the first farmers toiled the land or grazed their sheep on these ancient hills near Guiting Power?

History of the Farm Park

The foundations of the Cotswold Farm Park were laid more than 70 years ago in Blitz-ravaged London. My dad, Joe Henson, grew up in a theatrical family amid all the glitz and the glamour of show business. But his heart lay elsewhere. His toy set of lead animals and his regular visits to a neighbouring dairy farm were a sure sign of the career to come.

Dad settled in Gloucestershire in 1962 to work in partnership with his old school friend John Neave. They were looking for a venture they could run between them and Dad was working locally when he heard about a small, traditional Cotswold farm not far from Bourton-on-the-Water. In those days Bemborough Farm was just 160 hectares (400 acres), a quarter of what it is today. The land was owned by Corpus Christi College, Oxford; one of England's great seats of learning with a worldwide reputation for specialising in the classics. Past graduates include a former Poet Laureate, Robert Bridges, the ex-Agriculture Minister William Waldegrave and more recently, both Ed and David Miliband. Corpus Christi offered Dad something that's unheard of today - a three generation tenancy.

The new arrivals set to work on what was first and foremost an arable farm, earning their living from growing and selling wheat and barley.

Dad with Oxen in the early days

It wasn't long before that lifelong love of traditional farm stock led to the arrival of a flock of rare breed sheep. The first small steps (or perhaps hoof prints) towards the Cotswold Farm Park we see today.

Joe Henson and the Rare Breeds Survival Trust (RBST)

My parents on the day Dad got his MBE

The creation of the Cotswold Farm Park coincided with a growing realisation that traditional breeds of British farm animals had been neglected for far too long. For decades they had been regarded as old fashioned and outmoded. Dad remembers a time when even one of today's most popular breeds was treated with derision: "*I would take my Old Spot Pigs to Gloucester livestock market and people just stood and laughed. They thought I was joking*". It was that sort of attitude which had caused more than 20 British breeds to go the way of the Dodo and the Great Auk and become extinct in the years since 1900.

But the tide was turning. A living 'gene bank' of breeding sheep and cattle had been set up and in 1969 Dad became the first chairman of the Rare Breeds Survival Trust (RBST), dedicated to saving and promoting our indigenous cattle, sheep, pigs, goats, poultry, horses and ponies.

A phone call from a TV producer led to the first of many appearances on the children's show 'Animal Magic' with the legendary Johnny Morris. Soon Dad became BBC Bristol's 'tame farmer' and began working for the world-famous Natural History Unit, as well as popping up on other TV and radio programmes, including 'Blue Peter' and 'In The Country' with Angela Rippon and Phil Drabble.

In the Queen's Birthday Honours of 2011 Dad was recognised for services to conservation and I felt extremely privileged to watch him receive the MBE from Princess Anne at Windsor Castle. As I'll tell anyone who asks - he's not just my dad, he's also my **mentor and my hero**.

“I’m an animal anorak, I always have been”

Joe Henson

The Development of the Cotswold Farm Park

We've come a long way in the four decades since the gates of the Cotswold Farm Park were initially opened to the public. Those first visitors in 1971 were treated to the Henson collection of the three county breeds; Gloucester cattle, Old Spot pigs and a little flock of Cotswold sheep which belonged to my sister, Libby. On day one, this trio of breeds was joined by Highland, Longhorn, White Park, Belted Galloway and Dexter cattle. While the sheep pens also included Jacobs, Soays, Portlands and a single Norfolk ram. Some of the animals had come from Whipsnade Zoo which had decided to sell its 'gene bank' of British livestock.

As the years rolled by more people experienced foreign holidays and their expectations grew. So we've always tried to keep ahead of the trends by bringing in new breeds and attractions, developing the touch barn, improving our lambing, milking and shearing demonstrations, providing a shop and a high quality café. In the past few years we've started hosting events and festivals and recent innovations include the 'Rare Breeds Through History Trail' and audio guide which follows the story of farm animals from our ancient ancestors right up to the modern day.

In the Farm Park's first year we had 20,000 visitors which Dad thought was the most we'd ever get. But now we welcome more than 80,000 people every spring and summer.

Together Dad and John Neave had built fences and arranged toilet facilities, while my mum made sandwiches and cups of tea which she served from a caravan.

Adam's early years

Even when I was a nipper it was obvious that I would follow Dad into farming. As soon as he left the house every morning to muck out the pigs or repair the tractor, I'd be pulling on my little wellies to chase him across the yard.

I was brought up in the farmhouse where I now live with my family and in fact my son, Alfie, sleeps in my old bedroom. The circle of life and all that! In other professions they warn you against 'living over the shop' but when your home and workplace is as beautiful as this, it's no hardship whatsoever.

But the bright lights of television were never far away. As a kid I was used to seeing TV crews on the farm and Dad was always being interviewed for the news or wildlife programmes. Although for a real glimpse of the limelight I'd have to wait for a visit from Uncle Nicky. The theatrical gene may have bypassed Dad but his brother makes up for it. Nicky is a Shakespearean actor and a familiar face in TV dramas like 'EastEnders', 'Casualty' and 'Downton Abbey'. Despite that, his most famous role must be the medallion-wearing womaniser Mr Johnson in an episode of 'Fawlty Towers'. In the early 1970s he was married to Una Stubbs (who starred in 'Summer Holiday' and 'Worzel Gummidge'), so our family Christmases were a riot of parlour games and showbiz gossip.

Me (right) aged 5 with my sisters

Travelling with Duncan, aged 21 in 1998, Australia

Learning about Merino sheep in Australia

The glorious Gloucestershire countryside has always been home to me and although I've travelled the world, I wouldn't swap the Cotswolds for anything.

The Team

You can point at Bemborough Farm on a map. You can read about it in guide books and even see it every Sunday on national television. But the heart of the Farm Park isn't the fields or the buildings – it's the people who make it tick.

We have a full time crew of ten who work on site all year round and they're joined by another 50 seasonal staff who come on board for the busy spring and summer period. They help care for the livestock, look after the ticket office, run the restaurant and manage the gift shop. Most of them live in the towns and villages of the Cotswolds, so the annual visitor season makes us a significant local employer.

Since our opening day in 1971 we have striven to treat every visitor as a personal guest. I'm proud to say that it's a philosophy which every member of the team takes very seriously. Over time that caring attitude and attention to detail has helped us win many accolades including a Gold Cotswold Tourism Award for Attraction of the Year.

I look at the Farm Park staff as more than just workers. They're a brilliantly dedicated team who are extremely knowledgeable about the animals, passionate about the rare breeds movement and great ambassadors for tourism in the Cotswolds.

My name might be on the sign above the entrance but the place would be nothing without them.

Duncan & team

Meet Duncan Andrews. I've known him since the 1980s when we were both agricultural students at Seale Hayne College near Newton Abbot. Somehow I convinced him that helping me revise for my exams was a brilliant thing to do and we've remained great friends to this day.

Dunc is my business partner and runs the farm with me in a straight 50/50 split. Although you won't see this Scilly Islander on the telly very often, I'm the first to admit that he's the real business brain behind the farm operation. Not only can he operate a combine harvester and rebuild a lambing shed but he also has an in depth knowledge of agricultural science and rural commerce. He's constantly watching the latest developments, worldwide trends, commodity prices and exchange rates. In fact just being with him can be exhausting!

We've worked together in the Cotswolds since 1997 and his judgement has always been spot on. Together we're building on half a century of family heritage here at Guiting Power and making a commitment to run the business to the highest possible standards. In fact we've all pledged to support the nation's food producers, encourage localness and ensure integrity, honesty and good quality in everything we do. We call it '**Passion in British Farming**'.

Duncan and I are supported by a fantastic team of talented managers and staff who work on the farm and at the Farm Park.

Farming

The commercial farm

Bemborough Farm is my home, my playground and, importantly, my work place too. Long before it became one of Britain's best known farms thanks to our weekly adventures on 'Countryfile', this place earned its keep as a commercial arable and livestock operation. That's still the case today with more than half the 650 hectares (1600 acres) used for growing food and fuel; mainly winter barley, wheat, oilseed rape and beans. These are crops which help to make bread, biscuits, beer, cooking oil, biofuel and animal feed.

The local landscape is famous for its soft, gentle appearance but get a little closer and you realise that the soil around here is thin and stony. It's known as Cotswold brash and it's renowned among growers for its poor quality. So what Mother Nature lacks, we have to make up for as best we can. After all, we rely on the soil to produce all our crops and grass. We manage the fields carefully, measuring the natural nutrients and helping their growing potential by applying just the right amount of fertiliser for every part of the farm. Below the surface it's essential to look after the soil structure by allowing worms to move freely and encourage microorganisms to nourish the earth. So we rotate our crops and work the land with care to avoid compressing the soil.

Alongside the arable farm we have 243 hectares (600 acres) on which we graze all our rare breeds and a flock of 350 commercial sheep to produce lamb for the table. We put the rams with the ewes in the autumn, they give birth in the spring and we're able to sell the lambs from the middle of July right through until December.

Bemborough is too small to keep up a constant supply of meat to the supermarkets, so we've joined forces with 100 other farmers to create the Cotswold Lamb Group. Between us we produce about 150,000 animals every year.

The farming year

Whether you rear livestock or grow crops, successful farming depends on the seasons and knowing what to do and when to do it (with some decent weather and a little bit of luck thrown in). But it's worth remembering that the agricultural year doesn't necessarily chime with the calendar year. January and February are quiet months on the land and usually the darkest, coldest time of the year too. Apart from pruning, coppicing and perhaps some crop spraying to prevent disease, it's a chance for many hard-working farmers to catch their breath.

So the annual farming cycle really begins when the warmer weather and longer days arrive in March. That's the time for planting spring cereals like wheat, barley and oats as well as the arrival of new borns in the animal sheds. You know the season's underway when you catch the sight of a lamb, goat kid or calf stumbling to its feet for the first time.

If you've never seen a sheep being sheared at the Cotswold Farm Park, you've missed a treat. From the beginning of May until early July, thousands of visitors watch spellbound as our ewes and rams are treated to their annual short back and sides. It's a scene that's repeated on sheep farms all over the country. Now I like to think I'm quite good with the electric clippers but I'm a slow coach compared to the professionals, especially the Australian shearing gangs who visit Britain every year. They can get a fleece off in one piece in less than a minute.

Perhaps the best-known farming activity of the year is the harvest. Everybody knows about the gathering in of the crops but harvest time isn't confined to the month of August. British farmers are harvesting crops of one sort or another from late May all the way through to September and into October. It begins with early strawberries, followed by salad vegetables, cherries and gooseberries and by the time July arrives the machinery is in the fields bringing in oilseed rape, barley and wheat. The next couple of months are when you're most likely to see a farmer with his fingers crossed, in the hope of dry, sunny weather to help the combine harvesters work the fields.

As the days shorten and autumn creeps in, ploughing gets underway in earnest, cattle are housed indoors for the winter and it's time for tupping. This is when the ewes are mated with the ram for spring lambing the following year. Soon all the winter veg will be picked, the Christmas fat stock sales will be over and the farming cycle will begin again.

Arable equipment

It's been a very long time since the entire population of a village would turn out to bring in the harvest. Today's arable farmers employ relatively few staff but use hi-tech, super-efficient machinery instead. Much of this agricultural hardware can be described as a massive computer on wheels. Electronic sensors, roof-top satellite receivers and in-cab touch screens are the norm these days. So you can imagine that this kind of equipment doesn't come cheap. The type of combine harvester we use every summer costs around £250,000 brand new and even second hand ones sell for more than £100,000. Understandably tractors, cultivators, fertiliser spreaders, sprayers and combines are often shared between neighbouring farms to ease the cost of owning and running the equipment.

There's also a knock-on benefit for the environment as modern diesel tractor engines produce just 1% of the emissions that their equivalents did in the 1990s.

Rare Breed Collection

Pigs

Pick up a book, watch TV or go to the movies and it seems that pigs are everywhere, from Napoleon in George Orwell's 'Animal Farm' to Miss Piggy in 'The Muppets'. But how many people realise the heritage of Britain's native pig breeds? They originated as 'free-range' livestock, roaming through the forests being herded by ancient farmers. If you want to know what those swine herds were like, look no further than the Iron Age pigs at the Farm Park. In 1973 Dad crossed Tamworth sows with European wild boar. The delightful piglets were born with stripes from nose to tail and proved an instant success. Today there are rare and lovely varieties like the little Berkshire, the docile British Saddleback, Large Blacks with their big lop ears, Middle Whites famous for their tiny snouts and the perfectly pear-shaped Welsh.

Perhaps the most popular and easily recognised breed is the Gloucestershire Old Spot. The ever-present black patches on their backs give them away. They're lovely, laid-back animals and originated in the Severn Vale where they would clear the orchards of windfall apples and pears. But don't get caught out by the old wives' tale that their distinctive spots are bruises caused by falling fruit.

Sadly some British pig breeds have become extinct. We'll never see another Cumberland, Lincolnshire Curly Coat or Dorset Gold Tip. But hopefully Britain's new-found interest in farming and the hard work of the RBST means the future's bright for the rest.

Gloucestershire Old Spot

"Dogs look up to us, cats look down on us but pigs treat us as equals"

Winston Churchill

Cattle

There's so much more to cattle than just hides, horns and hooves. The British landscape would be unthinkable (and very overgrown) without them. Our kitchens would be pretty empty too. Over the centuries we've used cattle for providing milk, beef and leather as well as working livestock pulling ploughs or harvest wagons. In fact it's thought the last working team of oxen on a British farm were employed on the Bathurst Estate in Cirencester before the Second World War. But around the world oxen are still a familiar sight particularly in Asia and Africa.

Today the most common breed of cow in Britain is the Holstein-Friesian. They're just about everywhere and they're renowned for their black and white markings as well as their high milk yield. But despite their popularity they're not a traditional British breed, originating instead in the Netherlands. On this side of the Channel a diverse and colourful collection of domestic livestock has evolved. A roll-call of just some of our native cattle reads like an atlas of the British Isles; Aberdeen Angus, Ayrshire, Devon, Belted Galloway, Gloucester, Guernsey, Hereford, Highland, Lincoln Red, Shetland, Sussex and Welsh Black. Breeds as varied as the British countryside itself and every one perfectly suited to its original region and the needs of the local farmers.

Belted Galloway

Shetland lamb

Sheep

Large but docile with mild, kindly-looking eyes and wool that's thick, lustrous and smooth to the touch. That's a depiction any sheep would be proud of but in this case it describes the Cotswold. In fact their fleece is so lovely that in the Middle Ages it became an international commodity bringing massive wealth to the region. To this day magnificent medieval churches with large towers are referred to locally as wool churches. But tastes changed and Cotswold sheep fell out of favour so much that by 1950 there was only one purebred flock left.

The Cotswold is a family favourite but there are other breeds which help tell the story of our native livestock. Think of rare breed sheep and many people will picture the Jacob. Spotted and sporting anything up to six horns, this is a breed so old that it's thought to have provided the wool for the biblical Joseph and his coat of many colours. Then there's the comical-looking Kerry Hill with its white fleece and startling black eye patches, ears, nose, knees and feet.

We have a further 10 breeds at the Cotswold Farm Park and they're displayed in chronological order to explain the way man has domesticated animals through the ages. From the Neolithic Soay and the Bronze Age North Ronaldsay to the breeds of the invading Vikings and Normans; Hebrideans, Manx Loghtans, Norfolk Horns and Herdwicks. The story takes us through Tudor times and beyond with Portlands, White Face Dartmoors and Castlemilk Moorits then on to a modern commercial breed, the Texel.

"In Europe the best wool is English and in England the best wool is Cotswold"

12th century saying

Horses & ponies

It wasn't so long ago that horses and ponies were part of British working life. The big powerful Clydesdale and Suffolk Punch ploughed the fields, the majestic Shire drew the brewer's dray and the perky little Welsh Mountain pony was perfect on postal routes or pulling carts in the coal mines. Our lifestyles have been transformed in the last 100 years and very few equines are used in industry today. But it's no coincidence that we still describe a busy and reliable piece of machinery as the 'workhorse' of an organisation.

Back in 1983 my dad made a Radio 4 series called 'Natural Selection' in which he investigated man's relationship with various animals. One programme was devoted to the horse and he introduced listeners to 'Crusader', his Exmoor pony and the Farm Park's herd sire that year. This friendly young stallion was a great example of the oldest horse breed in Britain and possibly the most ancient domestic breed in the world. Exmoors have all the tell-tale primitive markings – the light colouring around the nose, a black mane and tail, fleshy eyelids and occasionally you can see a little bit of striping on the legs of the foals. They also have extremely hard feet (because primitive horses don't need to be shod).

Spotted pony

Poultry

How about this for a mind boggling fact - there are more chickens in the world than humans and although we'll never know the exact figure, it's believed there are around 11 billion fowls on the planet. Luckily for us, the poultry family tree is pretty healthy and we've got scientific proof that the chickens we see in coops and farmyards today are directly descended from the Red Jungle Fowl. It's a shy game bird from Southern Asia that's a member of the tropical pheasant family.

The word poultry covers a wide (and very colourful) array of creatures including turkeys, ducks, geese, guinea-fowl, peacocks and the most popular species of all, chickens. Our ancient ancestors used chickens for cock fighting and in rituals so we didn't start eating them until the Roman invasion in 43 AD. Our chicken rearing and eating habits changed very little between then and the end of the Second World War when intensive poultry farming began in earnest.

At the Farm Park we're very proud of our British poultry breeds like the Light Sussex, Scots Dumpy and the Brecon Buff goose. But for people who love local breeds, there is a Gloucestershire variety of waterfowl; the Khaki Campbell duck was developed by Adele Campbell in her orchard at Uley in 1901. Indian Runners were bred with Rouens and then crossed with Mallards to produce this placid little bird.

Khaki Campbell duckling

They make wonderful pets and are prolific egg layers. Great news if you like an omelette for breakfast.

Other animals

Magnificent bulls and mighty heavy horses might delight photographers and film-makers but there's more to traditional livestock than just the big boys.

Goats are amongst the most characterful of all farm creatures as anyone who's had their coat or handbag nibbled will testify! Our rarest domestic breed is the beautiful Golden Guernsey which owes its survival to the late Miriam Milbourne. She courageously hid the last remaining herd in a cellar during the Nazi occupation of the Channel Islands in World War Two. The striking black and white Bagot is another goat with an impressive family tree; Richard the Lionheart brought them to Britain after the crusades in the 12th century and later Richard II gave the Royal Herd to Sir John Bagot of Blithfield Hall near Rugeley as a reward for a good day's hunting in the Staffordshire countryside.

People are often surprised at the wide variety of animal species at the Farm Park. It's home to some very friendly donkeys, as well as African geese and even the occasional guinea-fowl.

As the name suggests, the Touch Barn is the place where kids (and grown-up kids) can stroke and hold the animals. It's also where you'll see piglets and lambs which need a little extra care and attention from the Farm Park staff.

Over the years the Touch Barn has become a wonderful place of discovery for generations of families and it's heart-warming to see how handling a small animal for the first time can bring sheer delight to the faces of young and old alike.

If it's a close encounter with rabbits, guinea-pigs or chicks you want, then head for the ever popular Touch Barn.

Rare Breeds Through History Trail

The livestock we keep in fields and paddocks today are descended from animals that our ancestors would have reared and herded. The breeds you can see at the Farm Park can be traced to every period of history, from ancient Britain and the Roman occupation, to the Middle Ages and the Victorian era. Across the centuries sheep, cattle, pigs and horses have all played their part in the story of man and the land. Their tales are told in a fascinating timeline and a series of listening posts called the 'Rare Breeds Through History Trail'.

Modern farming and the future 1960 - 2020

The explosion in world population and the increasing demands on economic and environmental resources have led to some of the most significant technological advances ever seen in farming. Efficiency, environment and welfare remain the priorities for farmers in the UK, but a global marketplace and a demand for cheap food continues to put pressure on systems and force innovation in the production of food and energy.

Texel sheep

Wheat crop

Crop science and biotechnology allow greater yields to be produced with lower inputs.

Wildlife areas are created on farmland to balance delicate ecosystems and preserve and protect our native species.

We are much more interested in the sources of our food, and demand for organic, locally grown and rare breed produce increases.

Holstein Fresian cow

UK Population 62 Million Predicted 67 Million by 2030.

1950 The first bull semen is frozen at Cambridge University.

1955 Fast food outlets appear across the country.

1969 First men on the moon.

1996 Dolly the sheep is created as an identical clone to another animal.

2001 Foot and Mouth disease cripples the livestock industry, with knock on effects to the rural economy and tourist industry.

2020 Agriculture is an exciting place to be. Farmers need to be hard working, entrepreneurial, innovative and technologically minded to meet the demands of today, whilst preserving our natural resources for future generations.

Food

Everyone loves a biscuit with their mid-morning cuppa, but how many people realise that their favourite cookie may well have started life at Bemborough Farm? We grow hundreds of acres of wheat. Once the grain has been harvested it's sold to the big commercial bakeries to be used for making biscuits as well as bread. Wheat is one of our traditional crops but in the 1970s a new and vibrant colour was added to the patchwork palette of the British landscape. Bright yellow rapeseed flowers appeared for the first time and it's now become the country's third most widely grown arable crop. Rapeseed oil is so versatile, being used in everything from candles and soaps to plastics and biofuel. In recent years our rapeseed has been used to make R-Oil, a natural, healthy cooking oil and salad dressing produced in the Cotswolds. It's delicious and it's even giving olive oil a run for its money.

A field full of ripe, golden barley shifting in the breeze is a beautiful sight. This is a crop that's destined for the brewing trade. Now when I was an agricultural student I got to know quite a bit about beer! But I never thought that one day I'd actually be producing my own ale. Thanks to the addition of Herefordshire hops and Mendip spring water plus a lot of hard work by Butcombe Brewery, my Maris Otter malting barley is now used to make a refreshing premium bitter.

We work closely with local suppliers like Anna MacCurrach from LoveMyCow and Rob Rees, The Cotswold Chef.

The name of the beer? Well it could only be 'Adam Henson's Rare Breed'.

Food

Man has been working with livestock since pre-historic times. The vast majority of the farm animals we know today were developed or domesticated to provide us with one of three things; power through creatures like plough oxen and heavy horses, fibre such as sheep's wool or food like milk and meat.

Every farmer cares for the health and welfare of his flock or herd but when you rear livestock for food there's no room for sentimentality when the time comes to send them to the abattoir. A scheme to promote rare breeds meat was originally set up by the Rare Breeds Survival Trust (RBST) and in 2003 it became the Traditional Breeds Meat Marketing Company run by a knowledgeable and enthusiastic Gloucestershire character called Richard Lutwyche. He provides the link between the farmer, accredited butcher's shops and the consumer. We've taken advantage of the scheme to sell pedigree rare breed pork, lamb, bacon and beef.

Traceability and localness is crucial if you want to maintain consumer confidence and we have a great working relationship with the butchers and farm shops who stock our meat. Lambourne's in Stow-on-the-Wold is our nearest outlet and they've even been featured on 'Countryfile'. They sell Bemborough Cotswold lamb, Old Spot pork and Gloucester beef. Further afield, some of our meat has become a bit of a delicacy in certain London restaurants.

The North Cotswolds Food and Farming Festival takes place at the Farm Park

Rare breed meat

We got some very strange looks when we first suggested that Britain's rare breeds could be saved by eating their meat. The idea isn't as daft as it sounds of course. It's called conservation through consumption and it's all about creating a demand for rare breeds meat; if people get a taste for White Park beef or Tamworth ham then more butchers will stock the products and in turn more farmers will rear the breeds.

Thankfully consumers have now woken up to the wonders of these traditional, local, sustainable and often free range or organic foods. There's a real market for lamb joints, pork chops, sausages, pies, burgers, bacon and even potted beef from rare breeds. What's more, they've moved from being a peculiarity stocked by specialist dealers to become a common sight at farm shops, farmers' markets, high street butchers and supermarket delis.

Don't just take my word for it. Rare breeds meat has earned the support of some of the best known chefs on British television including John Torode, Rick Stein and the Hairy Bikers. The food industry now recognises that there really is something special about the slow maturing, often fattier and certainly flavoursome meats which intensive farming left behind in the post war years. Now there are books dedicated to the subject, website recipes and even rare breeds cookery classes at the Three Counties Show.

Dad and me at market

If you've never tasted Old Spot pork or Gloucester beef, why not give them a try? You'll never look back.

Beef and Ale Pie

1 kg Rare breed beef, cut into 2cm cubes
5 tablespoons R-Oil or beef dripping
30g plain flour
30g unsalted butter
225g of mushrooms, quartered
3 or 4 carrots in chunks
2 onions thinly sliced
1/2 teaspoon sugar
400 ml of Rare Breed ale
300ml beef or chicken stock
3 sprigs thyme
3 bay leaves
Tablespoon Worcestershire sauce
800g puff pastry (preferably homemade!)
A little beaten egg for brushing

Serves 6

Season the beef with salt and pepper and lightly roll in the flour. Shake off, but keep the excess flour.

Heat three tablespoons of R-Oil (or beef dripping) in a large saucepan and brown the meat on all sides. Transfer to a plate.

Heat another tablespoon of oil and half the butter in the pan, fry the mushrooms briefly, transfer to a plate. Fry the carrots for a couple of minutes lightly.

Add more oil and the rest of the butter, add the onions and sugar and fry over a medium heat until they are softened and lightly browned.

Stir in the remaining flour and gradually add the ale and stock and bring to the boil, stirring.

Return the beef, mushroom and carrots to the pan with the thyme, bay leaves and Worcester sauce. Cover and simmer for 1 1/2 hours until the meat is still tender. Stir occasionally.

Line a deep pie dish with pastry, letting a little hang over the edge. Preheat the oven to 200c/400f/gas mark 6

Lift the meat, onions and vegetables out of the pan and put into the pastry dish.

Take out the bay leaves and reduce the remaining liquid. Pour into the pie. Brush the edges of the pastry with some beaten egg.

Roll out the remaining pastry and carefully place it as a lid over the pie. Crimp it together to seal.

With a sharp knife cut a small cross in the centre of the pastry lid.

Brush with beaten egg and bake for 30-35 minutes until the pastry is golden and the juices are bubbling hot. Serve with mash or boiled buttered potatoes and steamed spring greens.

It's simple, delicious and a favourite in the Henson household.

BUTCOMBE
Adam Henson's
Rare Breed
BUTCOMBE
West Country Bitter

Environment

The public image of farming has been turned on its head in the last twenty years. The old stereotype of a shotgun-wielding misery yelling "get orf my land" has been replaced by a more realistic picture of a caring, conservation-minded professional. And it's all down to the environment.

Long gone are the days when most farmers destroyed hedgerows, ploughed meadows, grubbed up traditional orchards and sprayed poisonous insecticides like DDT around without a second thought. Through incentives and a gradual awakening of the environment consequences, we've gone from simply using the land for our own means to becoming custodians of the countryside.

So now the modern farmer actively encourages birds, insects, amphibians and all kinds of native wild plants by working with nature. Across the country we're restoring orchards, building beetle banks, planting new woodland, reviving flower-rich hay meadows, digging ponds, using local building materials and leaving strips of uncultivated land at the edges of our fields (called margins). Together they provide food, shelter and breeding habitats for a whole range of wildlife; farmland birds like goldfinches and meadow pipits, barn owls, dormice, native butterflies, beetles and even natterjack toads.

Farming with the environment isn't just concerned with wildlife. It's about protecting local rivers and streams by avoiding pollution and making sure the air is as clean as possible. This is done by cutting emissions from machines and nourishing the soil with more natural waste.

Environment

When the word biodiversity was first being used by TV naturalists like David Attenborough and David Bellamy, few of us knew what they were talking about. But now we understand the benefits of creating landscapes and habitats that encourage a wide variety of life forms. That's certainly something we strive to do on the farm and we've had some incredible results.

The beautiful limestone grassland to the south of the Farm Park is alive with native plants, birds and butterflies which can be found in abundance and it's thought the area supports 100 species of wildflowers and grasses alone. Cowslips and early purple orchids thrive in the spring while kidney vetch, harebells and field scabious flower in the summer. Not to mention green-winged orchids, bee orchids, common restharrow and viper's bugloss.

It's not unusual to see roe deer and brown hare in the fields or to hear the lovely warbling song of the skylarks in flight.

You can enjoy all this on our two mile Wildlife Walk which takes you around a patchwork of fields and historic sites with such evocative names as Buttington, Stow Pitch and Tinker's Barn Ground. Arrows and information boards mark the route and you can pick up a Wildlife Walk map from the Farm Park shop.

Brimstone and orange-tip butterflies float on the first gentle breeze of spring and as summer approaches you can add the marbled white, the common blue and the small copper to your list.

The whole farm falls within the Cotswolds Area of Outstanding Natural Beauty (AONB). It's a status which is only one rung down the ladder from the National Parks like Exmoor, Snowdonia and the Lake District and means there are measures to protect the local landscape and its flora and fauna.

There's one corner of the farm which is particularly close to my heart. Barton Bushes is amongst Britain's very best wildlife locations and so in 1996 Natural England declared it an official Site of Special Scientific Interest (SSSI). The area is precious for two reasons. One is its population of the nationally scarce Duke of Burgundy butterfly. These small, delicate creatures have beautiful orange and brown wings with rows of white spots on the underside. If you're lucky you might see one perching on a leaf at the edge of the scrub.

The other rarity we've encouraged is a tiny plant with a lovely name; the Cotswold pennycress. Sure enough its grey-green leaves do look a bit like garden cress. The flowers are white and as they ripen, little heart-shaped seed pods form below the petals. As the name suggests, it's only found in the Cotswolds and even then it grows in just a handful of places.

The Cotswold pennycress is so rare that Parliament has given it legal protection in the Wildlife and Countryside Act.

Diversification

Have you ever wondered why so many farmers seem to busy themselves with small projects, cottage industries and rural businesses? Surely rearing livestock and growing crops is a full time job in itself. Well what those enterprising farmers have realised is that the key to successful and profitable agriculture in the 21st century is diversification. You can call it entrepreneurism, spreading the risk, having fingers in lots of pies or simply keeping your options open. But whatever label you put on it, diversifying your business is crucial if you want to balance the books at a time when earning a living from the land alone can be unreliable.

The idea took off in the 1970s when Farmhouse B&Bs started to spring up as people realised that spare rooms and converted barns could bring some money in. Fields and meadows became camp sites and before long more imaginative enterprises took off with farm shops, ice cream parlours and yoghurt production. More recently land and buildings have been used as rural retreats, workshops, yoga centres, museums and vineyards.

I suppose the prize for the most original diversification could be given to Somerset dairy farmer Michael Eavis. In 1970 he moved his cows off their pasture and invited rock bands and music fans to use the land for an outdoor concert. The admission fee was £1 which included free milk from Michael's farm. More than 40 years later the Glastonbury Festival is still going strong and it's become a multi-million pound affair.

The Cotswold landscape offers wide views and big skies - perfect for a canter or a gallop. Every year hundreds of people bring their horses to take part in our regular Sunday Fun Rides. The stunning 12 mile course includes more than 60 optional jumps and there's also a shorter route for the slightly less adventurous.

You could say that the Cotswold Farm Park is a classic example of diversification, although the prime reason for opening our gates to the public all those years ago was to share the Henson passion for traditional livestock and to make the case for Britain's rare breeds. We're proud to have been the world's first farm park but that doesn't mean we've stopped thinking of innovative ways of entertaining our visitors and engaging them with the countryside.

Back on the farm, the sheep shearing demonstrations are a great highlight every summer, but when the spectators have gone we don't throw the wool away. Our fleeces are sold to the British Wool Marketing Board which brings producers together and helps get them a better deal. We've also teamed up with a manufacturer who takes our wool to produce naturally-coloured goods like throws, cushion covers and picnic blankets for sale in outlets including the Cotswold Farm Park shop.

I'm a fervent campaigner for this home grown natural fibre but for years the industry was in the doldrums and it cost more to pay the shearing gang than we earned from selling the wool. Thankfully things are improving and wool prices have bounced back. So keep buying woollen socks, scarves and jumpers and look out for the Union Jack logo.

PASSION
IN BRITISH
FARMING
Adam Henson's
Cotswold
Farm park
Made with rare breed wool from
Adam Henson's
Cotswold
Farm park

Camping

The world famous Cotswolds offers a unique experience of the British countryside, combining beautiful villages, stunning scenery and unrivalled history. If you want to get a taste of this delightful corner of the country for yourself, then why not come and stay with us on the farm? We welcome tents, campervans, caravans and motor-homes on our campsite and with 40 pitches on the two acre site, there's plenty of room for you to make it a real home from home.

You'll be right on the doorstep for a day of fun at the Farm Park or you can use it as a base for exploring the Cotswolds and everything the area has to offer; the exciting attractions at Bourton-on-the-Water, art galleries and antiques shops in Stow-on-the-Wold, the great Roman settlement of Cirencester or the splendid Regency spa town of Cheltenham. We've worked hard to make our campers' stay as easy as possible with full facilities including showers and even a camp site shop for those last minute essentials. So what are you waiting for? Come stay and play.

Just imagine waking up to the sound of birdsong as the early morning mist drifts across the gentle rolling hills and the sun begins to rise over the stately beech trees on the horizon. While you cook breakfast in the open air, you could hear the bleating of new born lambs and if you're lucky, the distant chime of church bells.

JPM 831L

Playtime

There are times when children just want to let off steam by jumping, climbing or crawling about. So our adventure playground offers everything from an exhilarating zip wire to the ingenious giant jumping pillow – an attraction that's better than a trampoline and more fun than a bouncy castle. It's outdoor fun for everyone, as well as being healthy. The perfect way to fill your lungs with fresh Cotswold air!

Media

In 2001 'Countryfile' launched a competition to find a new presenter and after a big poke in the ribs from my partner, Charlie, I eventually sent a video to BBC Birmingham. Expecting to hear nothing I was gobsmacked when they invited me to an audition and I nearly passed out when they said I'd got the job! John Craven took me under his wing, showed this Cotswold farm boy the ropes and we've been best mates ever since.

Soon I was reporting on everything from Minke whales off the Isle of Mull and Hereford cattle in Australia to chicken racing competitions and the World Toe Wrestling Championships! Then in 2009 the programme moved from Sunday mornings to a peak time evening slot and the 'Adam's Farm' segment was born.

Along the way I've been lucky enough to present shows like 'Countryfile Summer Diaries', 'Lambing Live' with Kate Humble (and hundreds of sheep) as well as Radio 4 programmes such as 'On Your Farm'. We live in a multi-media world so I've spread my wings with a website, DVDs and monthly columns in 'BBC Countryfile' magazine and other publications like 'Cotswold Life'. So there were plenty of stories to tell when I was asked to write my first book; '**Adam's Farm: My Life on the Land**'.

I grew up watching John Craven on the telly and loved him on both 'Newsround' and 'Swap Shop'. But if you'd have told me then that one day I'd be appearing beside him on the box I'd never have believed it.

On set with my 'Countryfile' colleagues, Julia Bradbury, Matt Baker and John Craven

Make way for the moo-vie stars!

Almost as soon as the Farm Park was opened, the media began taking an interest in the animals. Perhaps it was the novelty factor at first, but it wasn't long before producers like Ken Jackson of BBC Radio Oxford and George Inger from 'Animal Magic' were taking rare breeds seriously and giving the Farm Park valuable airtime. It was fabulous publicity and people in the movie business began to sit up and take notice. For decades film producers had been working hard to get their sets right and ensure that actors and 'extras' wore accurate costumes and make up. Now they were turning their attention to the animal 'extras'. So Dad started hiring out period livestock for period films, because he had a breed of every species for every historical era.

It began when our Highland cattle and a small herd of goats were used for an ITV historical drama called 'Arthur of the Britons' with Oliver Tobias and Brian Blessed. Then in 1976 came our first experience of the big screen with the movie 'Joseph Andrews'. It was a rather racy 18th century costume comedy based on the Henry Fielding novel. The stars were Ann-Magret, Michael Hordern, John Gielgud and a young actor called Peter Firth in the title role. Much more recently Peter starred as Harry Pearce in the long-running TV series 'Spooks'.

The movie roles have kept on coming and over the years we've supplied period livestock for hundreds of productions. If you've watched 'Emma' with Gwyneth Paltrow, 'Robin Hood' starring Russell Crowe or Walt Disney's '101 Dalmatians' with Glenn Close, then you've seen some of the Farm Park's very own movie stars. We even supplied animals for the sci-fi film 'Alien 3'. It's nice to know that you're the first port of call when Hollywood needs Viking ponies, Mediaeval pigs or Victorian cattle (Exmoors, Tamworths and Belted Galloways respectively). I even managed to muscle in on the action myself when we helped the producers of the Mel Gibson film 'Braveheart'. If you're quick with the pause button and you look really closely you just might catch the sight of a familiar looking ginger-haired chap. I'm dressed as a filthy peasant leading the oxen which pull the cart carrying William Wallace's dead father back from battle. And who said the movies have lost their glamour?

Filming for 'Joseph Andrews' took place all over the West Country and particularly in Bath. Dad had to stock the lawn in front of the Royal Crescent with a mixed herd of Gloucester and Longhorn cattle and a flock of Cotswold sheep. It was quite a sight.

For two decades 'Countryfile' was a fixture of Sunday mornings on BBC One, championing rural life, gaining a loyal audience and getting pretty impressive viewing figures for that slot of around two million. So perhaps it shouldn't have been such a surprise when I was told that the programme was moving to primetime in 2009. Nevertheless I was concerned that a show which regularly featured reports on renewable energy, environmental issues and animal health was going to falter when we were put in competition with famous soap operas and glitzy game shows. I needn't have worried – straight away we were attracting up to seven million viewers a week and we soon became one of the most-watched factual programmes on British television.

Filming for 'Countryfile' has taken me from Cornwall to the Orkney Islands and virtually everywhere in between and I love being able to give a voice to Britain's farmers and to explore our agricultural heritage. 'Adam's Farm' has also reminded people about the beauty of the Cotswolds. The TV feature isn't meant to be a travelogue but hoteliers, B&B owners and tourism managers tell me that customers often say that their visit was prompted by long, lingering shots of local landscapes, villages and landmarks on 'Adam's Farm'. The TV programme is also great fun to make and I think that comes across on screen. What other job would see you judging livestock at the Three Counties Show, walking geese to market along the ancient drover's roads and leading a flock of Cotswold sheep through the streets of Stow-on-the-Wold to promote British wool?

Highland cattle are known for their strength and stamina and I needed a new bull to ensure the quality of the next generation of the herd at home. So the film crew followed me around the Spring Highland Cattle sale in Oban where some of the best examples of the herd were up for auction. Eric's powerful physique, straight legs and lovely upturned horns immediately caught my eye. I'd given myself a price limit and needless to say once he entered the sale ring I knew I was about to blow the budget. But he was worth every penny and Eric's appearances on 'Countryfile' certainly made an impression with the public because everywhere I go people ask after him.

In 2011 the show created a new animal 'celebrity' in the shape of Eric the bull. And what a shape! He's a ton of pure muscle with a leg in each corner.

The Future

So what does the 21st century hold for us? Well the future is definitely in farming with the world population expected to grow by two billion over the next 40 years. That's a lot of hungry mouths to feed which means that there'll be an ever increasing call for the crops we grow, the livestock we rear and the food technology we develop. Imagine the reaction of a website designer or a mobile phone manufacturer when told that their product will be in global demand in the coming years. That's why farmers who are open to new ideas and prepared to engage with the public have a very bright future indeed.

It'll not only mean working harder but also working smarter. That's where 'precision farming' comes in. Forget the Victorian labourer taking handfuls of seed and casting them across the field. Now satellite and computer technology can tell us exactly how much seed or fertiliser an area requires and precisely where it's needed. It saves time, waste and money. But not only are we using technology to produce food we are also farming energy by using wind, the sun and manure.

Despite the pressure on farms to turn on the tap for food production there is a renewed interest in local and provenance which is where Britain's rare and traditional breeds have their place. It's a delight to see Old Spot pork, Gloucester beef and Cotswold lamb appearing in butchers' shop windows and on restaurant menus once more. They taste delicious and the growing sales prove that I'm not the only one who thinks so.

It's a great time to be a farmer.

The return to traditional breeds

"These rare breeds are lovely to look at but they're just living museum pieces aren't they?" It's a question that I'm asked frequently and it's one that's easy to answer. Preserving rare breeds isn't about the past, it's about the future. Apart from providing an entertaining day out, the Cotswold Farm Park exists to ensure that the genes of our animals are conserved for the generations that follow.

Many traditional breeds of sheep, pig and cattle became rare because they weren't suited to intensive farming aimed at supplying mass markets; their meat didn't suit changing tastes, they were too expensive to rear or they simply didn't produce enough offspring to be profitable. But can we really afford to be complacent about letting them die out just because we can't find a commercial purpose for them at present? Once a rare breed is extinct it's lost forever. Keeping and breeding these animals is like having a genetic toolkit for the future; the biological building blocks that could help develop new livestock varieties, meet consumer demands and overcome disease in the decades to come.

Animals that, in some cases, have remained unchanged for thousands of years are vital if we're to understand our farming heritage, educate our children and aid research. If you want to find out more about the importance of Britain's native farm livestock, log on to the Rare Breeds Survival Trust website www.rbst.org.uk

Preserving rare breeds isn't about the past, it's about the future.

Renewable energy sources

The British countryside might have a quiet, rustic charm but in many places our fields and farms are helping to fuel the nation. Apart from growing food, modern farmers also have the capability to produce 'green' energy. Many have installed solar panels (or photovoltaic cells) to capture the power of the sun's rays. Large buildings like barns and animal sheds are perfect for this and the electricity generated is fed in to the National Grid. Perhaps more controversial are the increasing number of wind turbines being sited on farms. However, these are rarely seen in the Cotswolds, due to planning restrictions and the region's designation as an Area of Outstanding Natural Beauty (AONB).

Some farmers have been able to produce biogas by putting waste, manure or a range of crops in to a digester to produce methane. The gas is used to fuel a turbine and create electricity which, again, can be fed in to the grid. It's a fairly common way of generating energy on continental farms and increasingly the idea is being championed in this country.

Then there's biomass. This is energy produced from burning plant matter in biomass power stations. There are two main sources; either farming by-products, like straw, are used or specially grown crops like willow or poplar coppice are cut and chipped before being incinerated.

Miscanthus being harvested to create fuel briquettes.

Farming techniques

Our farming ancestors used basic methods to protect and promote their crops; some dug ditches to avoid flooding, others sowed two or three different plant seeds together in the same field to try to maximise the yield. In the 21st century farmers still want the same end result but now science and technology are on our side to make the task less unpredictable.

Nutrients in the soil are vital if you want to grow strong, healthy grain, fruit and vegetables and we can help things along by adding fertiliser. But thanks to the same satellite system that's used for in-car sat nav, we can now create a nutrient map of the land which helps us work out how much fertiliser we need to spread on different parts of the field. It's a bit of computer wizardry that makes the job kinder to the environment, cuts waste and saves both time and money.

Some farmers are now growing crops without soil at all. The hydroponic system is well established in Australia and it's led to things as diverse as barley, radishes and lettuce being grown in indoor trays with their roots in water that's rich with mineral nutrients. Not everyone is in favour of hydroponics but its supporters say it produces bigger yields, it's environmentally-friendly and it's easy to control pests.

The world population stands at more than seven billion and it's set to rise rapidly so scientists and agricultural-experts are under pressure to come up with new ways of improving and accelerating food production. In Britain that's something that must be done responsibly with careful consideration of the environment.

If you listen to 'Farming Today' on the radio or watch a news report about harvest on TV, you might hear someone described as an agronomist. In fact we employ one at Bemborough Farm. It simply means a person with expert knowledge in the science behind crop production and soil management (or agronomy).

Educating and engaging the public

Telling the story of British farming has been a large part of my life so it's exciting to discover that more and more people are eager to learn about agriculture. As we've become more informed about the food we eat, so we've begun to ask questions about things like the environment, sustainability, traceability, localness and food miles. There's growing public interest in farming practices, animal care, landscape and wildlife management. What's more, the UK's agricultural colleges are full again and they're training the next generation of farmers as well as agricultural professionals like food scientists, animal specialists and marketing experts.

So now the farming industry needs to keep that momentum going by continuing to be visible, open and honest. It's true that in the past British farmers didn't have a very positive reputation but that's changing. 'Open Farm Sunday' is a great example of how the industry is more confident about its achievements and proud of the highest hygiene and welfare standards in the world. But it needn't be confined to just one day in June. At home in the Cotswolds we're increasingly bringing the commercial farm on to the Farm Park. We're not only explaining rare breeds conservation to our visitors but also demonstrating modern agricultural methods and the ways we'll be farming in the future.

"In the end, we will conserve only what we love. We will love only what we understand. We will understand only what we are taught" *Baba Dioum, environmentalist*

Getting involved

If you've been inspired by the story of Britain's rare breeds why not take the next step and get actively involved? Don't panic, it doesn't mean rearing your own herd of Longhorn cattle - at least not straight away! But you can make a difference today.

You could begin by joining the Rare Breeds Survival Trust www.rbst.org.uk. It's a charity for anyone who's interested in preserving our unique rural heritage for future generations and there are local support groups all over the UK. The next time you're shopping, look out for rare breed meat and if you can't find Old Spot sausages or Cotswold lamb, you can help create a demand for it by asking the butcher to stock it for you. The same goes for British wool. If all the socks, scarves and gloves in your favourite clothes store are made from synthetic fibres or foreign wool, make your voice heard.

Back in the 1970s TV viewers laughed along with Richard Briers and Felicity Kendal in 'The Good Life' but time has finally caught up with the famous sit-com and rearing your own livestock is now more popular than ever. Keeping chickens is a great way to start. There's lots of advice and guidance available and once your hens start laying, you'll never have to buy eggs again.

We're proud to have been the first ever centre.